May your special angel
bless you today

To

From

Angels

Picture credits: **Denise Hilton Campbell; Christie s Images/Corbis; SuperStock:**
Christie's Images; David David Gallery; Charles Neal; Stock Montage.

Contributing writers: June Eaton, Lain Chroust Ehmann, Jan Goldberg,
Jennifer Ouellette, and June Stevenson

Book jacket illustrated by Robin Moro

New Seasons is a trademark of Publications International, Ltd.

Louis Weber, CEO
Publications International, Ltd.
7373 North Cicero Avenue
Lincolnwood, Illinois 60712

When God assigns your
guardian angel, it's a match
made in heaven.

*S*oft as a butterfly's wing grazing
your cheek is the caress of an angel
bringing you comfort.

A friendly voice in the dark of night,
The tentative rays of morning light,
A host of butterflies high in flight,
A rainbow extending far out of sight—
All these miracles tell me this:
Angels really do exist.

An angel is a friend on loan from heaven.

Each soft breeze is like the flutter of
angel wings passing you by. They are
God's reassurance that he is never
very far away.

Through the eyes of faith, I see the work of angels daily orchestrating my life on behalf of our heavenly Conductor.

Angels provide a heavenly view—
A God-sent message from him to you.

When we look with our
hearts, not our eyes, we will
see angels surrounding us at
every moment.

*I*t doesn't matter if we can't see angels. Our ability to feel their silent, supportive presence is a testament to our faith.

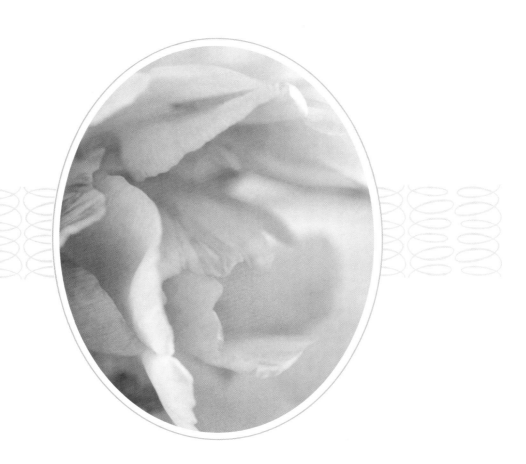

I prayed for an angel to comfort me at night.
I prayed for an angel to make the darkness bright.
When the long night was over and the pain was all gone,
I thanked God for the angel who kept me safe until dawn.

Angels change dusk to dawn.

Angels sing with the voice of
a laughing child and listen
with the ears of a wise mother.

Angels can be as nurturing as a mother
hen and as fierce as a father lion.
Like God, they embody the best of
female and male qualities.

An angel's wings are always large enough to shield the person they are sent to look after.

Angels don't fear the rain, snow, or stormy weather. They know their wings—and their spirits—are waterproof.

May you always travel with the wind at your back, a star for a compass, and an angel on your shoulder.

God's angels help us stay on a righteous path.

Sometimes it is only
after a crisis has passed
that we recognize that
angels have been present
all along.

Don't think you will find angels by looking heavenward. Most of them are making a difference in the lives here on earth.

Angels don't look at the
size of your purse
Nor measure your net worth.
Angels know you're precious
By virtue of your birth.

Angels are living examples that it's the size of your faith, not the size of your muscles, that determines your true strength.

Angels strengthen our spirits and soften life's blows.

Angels make us kinder and our lives more meaningful.

Angels are like smart
drivers. They know how to
put the brakes on our
impulsive behavior.
Sometimes they muffle
the sounds that distract us
from goodness, and they
always try to steer us in
the right direction.

*A*t work or at play,
Your guardian angel lights the way!

Angels do not just
guide and protect us;
they share the words
of our good Lord.

Angels help us see beautiful blooms in an overgrown
patch of weeds. And when our gardens are thriving,
they point toward the loveliness of creation in the
fragrance of each blossom.

Angels teach us how to listen, how to dream, and how to love.

God in heaven above,
Bless me with your love.
Send your angel choir to guide me.
Safe within your arms, please hide me.
High in heaven's dome,
I'll make your heart my home.

*I*f you feel as if you're floating on air, know that your guardian angel is upholding you.

*A*ngels lift our spirits by encouraging our hearts and
whispering words of faith into our ears.

An angel protects us from bad decisions, guides us through difficult situations, watches over us daily, and sends God's love when it seems no one else cares.

*I*n those mysterious, unexplained events of our lives, we sense the hand of an intervening angel to remind us of the reality of God's love.

Friend, confidant, advisor—
angels are whatever we
need them to be.

A friend who arrives at your door the precise moment you need her is certainly an angel sent from God.

There's no time to feel lonely when
we sense the presence of our
guardian angel.

We are always in God's sight;
His angels guard us day and night.
Their aid is always near
whenever dangers first appear.

God sends his angels to hold us
up so we don't stumble
in the darkness.

If you listen carefully during the long hours of a dark and lonely night, you may hear only silence. Angels do their work quietly, and when they are finished, they hurry away on tiptoe.

Angels are able to fly because they've emptied themselves of everything but love.

Angels fly at the speed of light when someone needs rescuing, and they keep their feet anchored to the ground when someone needs to be held.

What better measure of your heart
than your ability to see God's
angels around you?

Our belief in angels is evidence that the
longings of the spirit are more powerful
than the limitations of the mind.

Angels are like best friends—
They're here to listen and love us as we make our
way through the complications of life.

$\mathcal{W}$alking through life is much easier with
a guardian angel to lean on.

Angels remind us of the power of God.

Angels guide us through our day,
Making sure we find our way.
Angels guard us through the night,
Keeping us safe until the morning
light.

Angels are always beside us, rejoicing and laughing with us. And during hard times, they allow us to ride above our challenges on their wings.

No heart is so heavy and no
soul is so bleak that they can't
be lifted by the wings of angels.

Thousands of angels at God's command comfort, encourage, and guide us through the trials of our daily existence.

Angels lift our eyes heavenward especially
when troubles surround us.

Angels guide us in the here and now, so we may join them in the hereafter.

*May you always experience the presence
of angels in your daily life—that you
may have peace, comfort,
and hope for the future.*

When angels come, life's shadows leave.

Whether wide awake or
sound asleep,
Your guardian angel is
yours to keep!